North American
Animals

AMERICAN ALLIGATORS

by Steve Potts

Consulting Editor: Gail Saunders-Smith, PhD

CAPSTONE PRESS
a capstone imprint

Pebble Plus is published by Capstone Press,
1710 Roe Crest Drive, North Mankato, Minnesota 56003.
www.capstonepub.com

 Books published by Capstone Press are manufactured with paper
containing at least 10 percent post-consumer waste.

Library of Congress Cataloging-in-Publication Data
Potts, Steve, 1956–
  American alligators / By Steve Potts.
      p. cm.—(Pebble plus. North American animals)
  Includes bibliographical references and index.
  Summary: "Simple text and full-color photographs provide a brief introduction to American alligators"—Provided by
publisher.
  ISBN 978-1-4296-7703-5 (library binding)
  ISBN 978-1-4296-7918-3 (paperback)
  1. American alligator—Juvenile literature. I. Title.
  QL666.C925P687 2012
  597.98'40973—dc23   2011025650

Editorial Credits
Erika L. Shores, editor; Heidi Thompson, designer; Svetlana Zhurkin, media researcher;
    Kathy McColley, production specialist

Photo Credits
Dreamstime: Bill Swiger, 15; iStockphoto: Diane Stamatelatos, 21; Photolibrary: Alain Mafart-Renodier, 12–13;
Shutterstock: Ferenc Cegledi, 7, Heather Renee, 8–9, Heiko Kiera, 17, Kelly Laurent, cover, Michael J. Thompson,
18–19, Paul S. Wolf, 1, Tony Campbell, 5, VT750, 10–11

Note to Parents and Teachers

The North American Animals series supports national science standards related to life science.
This book describes and illustrates American alligators. The images support early readers in
understanding the text. The repetition of words and phrases helps early readers learn new
words. This book also introduces early readers to subject-specific vocabulary words, which are
defined in the Glossary section. Early readers may need assistance to read some words and to
use the Table of Contents, Glossary, Read More, Internet Sites, and Index sections of the book.

Printed in the United States of America in North Mankato, Minnesota.
102011   006405CGS12

Table of Contents

Living in North America

Dark eyes and round nostrils stick out of the water. It's an American alligator looking for food. These long animals are North America's largest reptiles.

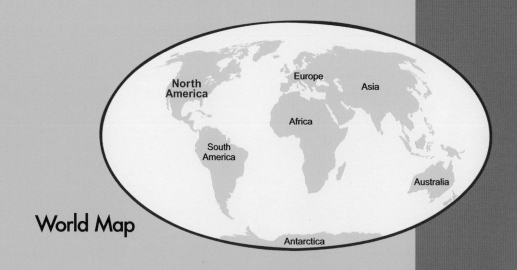

World Map

American alligators are found only in the southeastern United States. They live in wetlands, swamps, lakes, and other bodies of freshwater.

North America Map

where American alligators live

Up Close!

American alligators are gray-black. Their tough skin is covered with scales. Hard, bony plates called scutes grow on their backs.

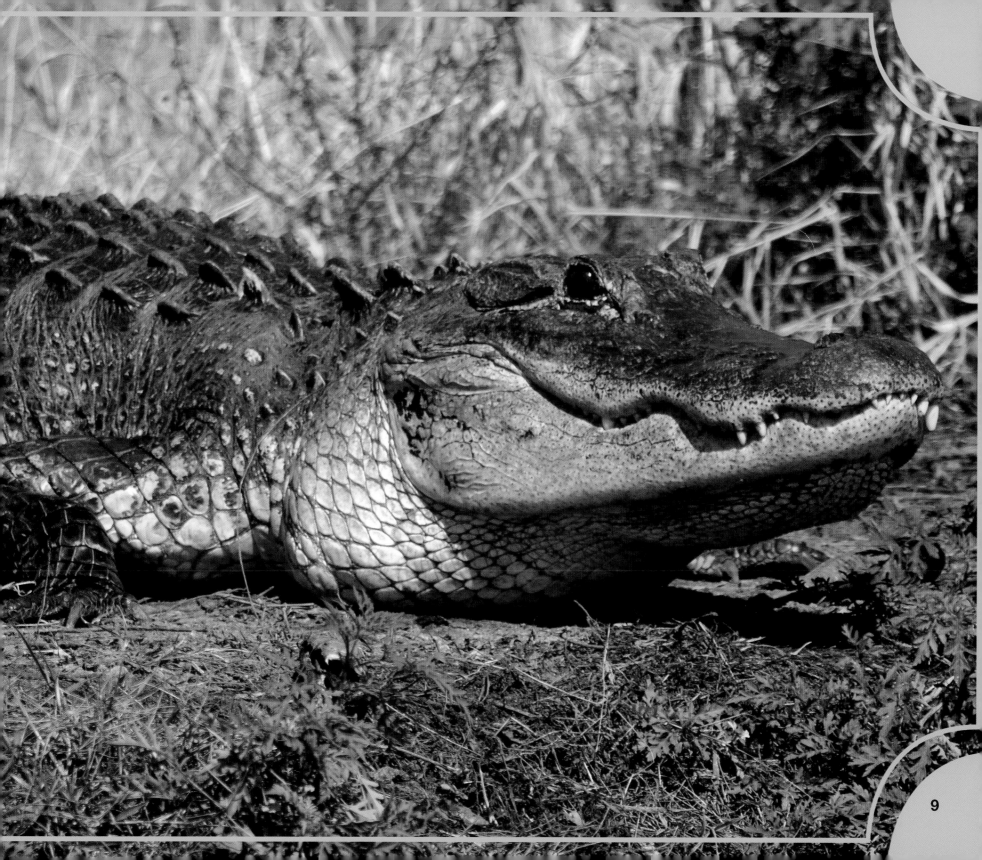

Alligators have short legs and long tails. Alligators grow up to 15 feet (4.6 meters) long. They weigh up to 1,000 pounds (450 kilograms).

Eating

American alligators will eat
almost anything.
They snap up birds, fish,
crabs, snails, turtles,
and other small animals.

With a snap of its jaws,

an alligator uses its 80 sharp

teeth to crush prey.

But it doesn't chew up the prey.

The alligator swallows it whole.

Growing Up

Alligators begin mating in April.
Females lay 20 to 50 eggs about
three weeks after mating.
Eggs begin hatching in August.

The newly hatched alligators
find their way to the water.
Mothers protect their young
from raccoons and snakes
during the first year.

Staying Safe

People are the only danger to adult alligators. Swampland disappears when people drain it to build homes. Setting aside land gives alligators space to live.

Glossary

hatch—to break out of an egg

mate—to join together to produce young

nostril—an opening in the nose used to breathe and smell

prey—an animal hunted by another animal for food

reptile—a cold-blooded animal that breathes air and has a backbone; most reptiles lay eggs and have scaly skin

scale—one of the small pieces of hard skin covering the body of an alligator, fish, snake, or other reptile

scute—a wide, bony plate on the back of an alligator

Read More

Feigenbaum, Aaron. *American Alligators: Freshwater Survivors.* America's Animal Comebacks. New York: Bearport Pub. Company, Inc., 2008.

Halfmann, Janet. *Alligator at Saw Grass Road.* Smithsonian's Backyard. Norwalk, Conn.: Soundprints, 2006.

Thomas, Isabel. *Alligator vs. Crocodile.* Animals Head to Head. Chicago: Raintree, 2006.

Internet Sites

FactHound offers a safe, fun way to find Internet sites related to this book. All of the sites on FactHound have been researched by our staff.

Here's all you do:

Visit *www.facthound.com*

Type in this code: 9781429677035

Check out projects, games and lots more at
www.capstonekids.com

Index

Word Count: 205

Grade: 1

Early-Intervention Level: 19